AMERICAN LEGENDS™

Casey Jones

Marianne Johnston

The Rosen Publishing Group's

PowerKids Press™

New York

Published in 2001 by The Rosen Publishing Group, Inc.
29 East 21st Street, New York, NY 10010

First Edition

Book Design: Michael de Guzman

Photo Credits: pp. 4, 12, 15, 16, 19 Courtesy of Historic Casey Jones Museum; p. 7 © Jim Cummins/FPG International; p. 8 © North Wind Picture Archives; p. 11 © Underwood & Underwood/CORBIS; p. 20 Courtesy of Springfield-Green County Library District.

Johnston, Marianne.
    Casey Jones / Marianne Johnston.
        p. cm.— (American legends)
    Includes index.
    Summary: This book describes the life and the legend of Casey Jones, the most famous train engineer in history.
    ISBN 0-8239-5582-6
    1. Jones, Casey, 1863–1900—Juvenile literature. 2. Locomotive engineers—United States—Biography—Juvenile literature. [1. Jones, Casey, 1863–1900. 2. Locomotive engineers.] I. Title. II. Series.
    2000
    363.1'22'0924—dc21
    [B]

Manufactured in the United States of America

Contents

This oil painting of John Luther "Casey" Jones is now in his historic home at the Casey Jones Home and Railroad Museum in Casey Jones Village in Jackson, Tennessee. It is said that as an engineer Casey liked to drive trains fast.

Casey Jones

The most famous train **engineer** in history was the great Casey Jones. He was a tall, strong man, with dark hair and gray eyes. No one could drive those huge, black, powerful **engines** like Casey. He drove them very fast, and was almost always on time. He loved to feel the wind on his face as he stuck his head out the window of his engine.

One night Casey saw another train stopped on the same track he was on. His train was going very fast, and he was afraid that he was going to crash into the other train. Casey tried to slow his train down, but he could not stop it in time. His train crashed into the other train. That horrible wreck made Casey Jones a **legend**.

What Is a Legend?

A legend is a story that has come down from the past. Sometimes we make heroes out of people who have qualities that we admire. Most people believe Casey Jones was a brave and **dedicated** engineer. Many people would like to be as brave as Casey Jones.

When a person's life has become a legend, the good qualities of that person become the center of stories about him or her. The stories grow more amazing and interesting with each telling. This **exaggeration** makes the legends more exciting. This helps us remember the good qualities of the **legendary** person.

Reading about legends, or stories that come down to us from the past, is fun. Legends are not always about real people or events from the past. Sometimes parts of the legends are made up to make the stories more exciting.

Engineers and firemen had important jobs on the railroad. The fireman rode in the cab of the train and shoveled coal under the boiler to keep the steam going. This powered the train. An engineer steered the train and knew how to control its speed.

Young Casey's Dreams

Casey Jones was born on March 14, 1863, although many people believe he was born in 1864. His real name was John Luther Jones. He was born in either Missouri or Kentucky. No one knows for sure.

When he was in his early teens, John and his family moved to the town of Cayce, Kentucky. The name of the town sounded just like the name "Casey." That is how John Luther Jones got his **nickname**, Casey. When he was still young, Casey wanted to be an engineer on a train more than anything else.

The History of the Railroad

When Casey was born, the train was still a new form of **transportation** in the United States. The first big railroad in this country, the Baltimore and Ohio Railroad, began in 1827. By the 1860s, there were railroads across most of the United States. As Casey grew up, trains quickly became more and more popular. Railroad tracks were laid down all the way to the western part of the United States. Trains made it much easier for people to get from one place to another. Trains were the fastest, newest, and best way to travel. Being a train engineer was a very exciting job.

This West Virginia railroad from around 1900 transported goods, such as coal, to people who needed them. Although many goods still traveled by boat, railroads were an important way of getting things to towns that were not located near rivers.

In this close-up view of Casey, he is in the cab of a train called the 638.
Casey became an engineer in 1890, when he was 27 years old.

Casey's Dreams Come True

Casey got his first job with the railroad in 1878, when he was only 15 years old. This job was in Columbus, Kentucky. He worked as a **telegrapher**. A railroad telegrapher's job was to send messages between trains and other railroad workers. Casey did not get to ride on the trains, though.

In 1887, Casey married Janie Brady from Jackson, Mississippi. They later became the parents of three children. When he was 25, Casey became a **fireman** for the Illinois Central Railroad. As a fireman, he shoveled coal into the hot stove of the train. The fire produced steam. This powered the train's engine and kept the train moving. When Casey was 27, his dreams of becoming an engineer finally came true.

A Great Engineer

Casey loved to drive his trains fast. He was known for always getting his engines in on time. Casey had a special way of tooting his trains' whistles. He would start the whistle very quietly, raise it up louder, and then slowly make it softer and softer until it stopped. The people who lived in the towns along Casey's routes would listen for this special whistle. When they heard it, they knew it was Casey Jones's train passing by.

In the beginning of 1900, Casey got his dream route. He became the engineer on train No. 1, the New Orleans Express, also known as the "Cannonball." This fast train ran from Memphis, Tennessee, to Canton, Mississippi.

Artist Jim Jordan's painting "A Tribute to Casey" shows the Mississippi countryside. Casey passed by this area of woods and ponds on his way to Memphis, Tennessee, when he drove the Illinois Central engine, known as the 382.

Sim Webb (top) was Casey's fireman on trains 638 and 382. He is seen here in a photograph that was taken many years after the April 30, 1900, train trip. He signed the photograph after it was taken and added the date of the wreck.

Casey's Last Run

On April 30, 1900, Casey made his last run as an engineer. He left Memphis very early in the morning. It was dark and rainy. He was already more than an hour late when he started his run. Casey drove very fast to make up time. He did not want to arrive in Canton, Mississippi, late. The train whizzed along the track at up to 100 miles (161 km) per hour.

At nearly four o'clock in the morning, on April 30, Casey's train was passing through Vaughan, Mississippi. Another train was stopped on the track. Casey and his fireman, Sim Webb, saw the **caboose** of the train ahead of them.

The Train Crash

Casey's train was going too fast to stop in time on that rainy morning in Mississippi. Casey pulled on the hand brake with all his might. He tried to slow down the train as much as he could. He yelled to Sim that he should jump from the train before it was too late. As Sim jumped, Casey blew on his whistle as loud as he could.

Casey's engine slammed into the caboose of the freight train on the track. Casey died in the fiery crash. Luckily, no one else was hurt too seriously. It is said that if Casey had not stayed on the train and held the brake to slow it down, more people would have died.

This painting by William George is called "The Crash Heard Around the World." It shows Casey's train wreck. Casey had taken the trip for an engineer who was sick. The train was running late, and Casey tried to make up the time by going fast.

Casey Jones

As Sung by Mr. T. R. Hammond in Osceola, Missouri on September 17, 1958

VERSES 1, 2, 3*, 4, 6, and 8

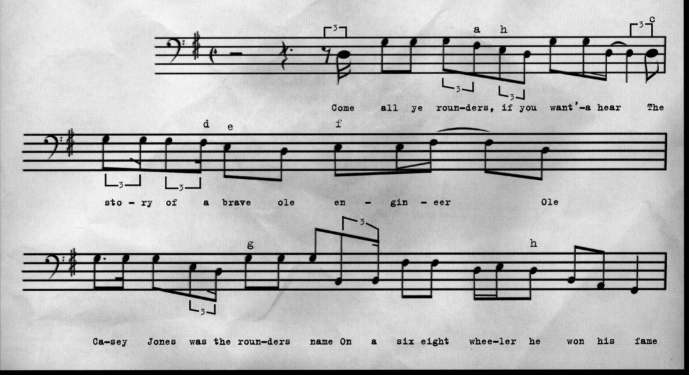

Wallace Saunders wrote "The Ballad of Casey Jones" soon after Casey died. Saunders had worked with Casey as an engine wiper and was his friend. The song became a hit. Over the years singers added verses to it, like the one seen here.

Casey Becomes a Legend

A man named Wallace Saunders was a close friend of Casey's. Wallace had worked at the railroad with Casey. He was very sad about Casey's death. He wrote a song called "The Ballad of Casey Jones" to honor his friend.

The song became very popular. People all across the country soon knew about Casey Jones. His legend grew as people added new verses to the song. Casey became the most famous railroad engineer of all time. Some of the new lines added to the song said Casey rode the rails all the way out west to San Francisco, California, and Salt Lake City, Utah. The real-life Casey never went west.

Remembering Casey Jones

Casey is buried in Jackson, Tennessee. You can visit Casey Jones Village in Jackson. The Casey Jones Home and Railroad Museum has an old engine that looks just like the one Casey drove. You can even go on board. On the museum's grounds you can also visit the house where Casey and his family once lived. The house was moved from East Chester Street in Jackson to the museum in 1980.

The town of Vaughan, Mississippi, also has a Casey Jones museum. It is called the Casey Jones Railroad Museum State Park and you can learn all about Casey's life and about the history of railroads in Mississippi there. The legend of Casey Jones still lives on today.

Glossary

caboose (ka-BOOS) The last car of a freight train that is mainly used by the crew of the train.

dedicated (DEH-dih-kay-tid) To have a special purpose.

engineer (en-jih-NEER) The person who drives the railroad engine.

engines (EN-jihnz) The powerful front cars of trains. An engine pulls the rest of the cars of a train along the railroad tracks.

exaggeration (ihg-zah-juh-RAY-shun) Something made to seem larger or more amazing than it really is.

fireman (FYR-man) A person who shovels coal into the hot stove of the engine, which makes steam and powers the train.

legend (LEH-jend) A story passed down through the years that many people believe.

legendary (LEH-jen-der-ee) To be based on a legend. Also, to be famous and important.

nickname (NIK-naym) A funny or interesting name given to a person that has something to do with that person's life.

telegrapher (teh-LEH-gra-fir) A person in charge of sending messages between people by using a telegraph. A telegraph is a device that sends coded messages over long distances, using wires and electricity.

transportation (tranz-per-TAY-shun) A way of traveling from one place to another.

Index

Web Sites

To learn more about Casey Jones and railroads, check out these Web sites:
http: //www.ksry.com/caseyjon.htm
http: //www.taco.com/roots/caseyjones.html
http: //146.7.8.8/folksong/maxhunter/0227/index.html